Investigate

Natural Resources

Louise Spilsbury

Heinemann Library
Chicago, Illinois

www.heinemannraintree.com
Visit our website to find out
more information about
Heinemann-Raintree books.

To order:

☎ Phone 888-454-2279

💻 Visit www.heinemannraintree.com
to browse our catalog and order online.

Edited by Siân Smith, Rebecca Rissman, and Charlotte Guillain
Designed by Joanna Hinton-Malivoire
Original illustrations © Capstone Global Library
Picture research by Elizabeth Alexander and Sally Cole
Originated by Modern Age Repro House Ltd
Printed and bound in China by Leo Paper Group

14 13 12 11 10
10 9 8 7 6 5 4 3 2 1

Library of Congress Cataloging-in-Publication Data
Spilsbury, Louise.
  Natural resources / Louise Spilsbury.
    p. cm. – (Investigate geography)
  Includes bibliographical references and index.
  ISBN 978-1-4329-3470-5 (hc) – ISBN 978-1-4329-3478-1 (pb) 1.
Natural resources–Juvenile literature. I. Title.
HC85.S656 2009
333.7–dc22
                              2009011044

Acknowledgments
The author and publishers are grateful to the following for
permission to reproduce copyright material: pp. **4** (© Robert
Harding Picture Library Ltd), **5** (© Roger Bamber), **18** (©
Wildscape), **19** (© F. Vrouenraths (Spain)), **21** (© Jack Sullivan), **27**
(© Superclic), **30 right** (© Roger Bamber); Corbis pp. **6** (© David
Vintiner/Zefa), **7** (© Moodboard), **13 right** (© Hall/Photocuisine),
15 (© Mark Bolton), **22** (© Andy Aitchison), **29** (© Bob Neimy/
AgStock Images), **30 left** (© David Vintiner/Zefa), **30 middle** (©
Mark Bolton); Getty Images p. **14** (DAJ); iStockphoto pp. **8** (©
Rachel Dewis), **10** (© Juanmonino), **11** (© Torsten Karock), **17**
(Maximillan Stock Ltd/Fresh Food Images), **20** (Maximillan Stock
Ltd/Fresh Food Images), **23** (PatitucciPhoto/OSF), **24** (Chad
Ehlers), **26** (Christopher Cormack/Imagestate), **28** (Ming Tang-
Evans/Fresh Food Images); Shutterstock pp. **12 left** (© Jagoush),
12 right (© Buquet), **13 left** (© Michael Effler), **16 bottom right** (©
Yellowj), **16 top right** (© Sandra Caldwell), **16 centre** (© Alexpi),
16 top left (© Arkady), **16 middle left** (© Elena Schweitzer), **16
middle right** (© Edyta Pawlowska); Still Pictures p. **25** (Sebastian
Laraia/Visum).

Cover photograph of men on a boat fishing reproduced with
permission of Corbis/© Philippe Giraud/Sygma.

Every effort has been made to contact copyright holders of
material reproduced in this book. Any omissions will be rectified in
subsequent printings if notice is given to the publishers.

Contents

Some words are shown in bold, **like this**. You can find out what they mean by looking in the glossary.

What Are Natural Resources?

Natural resources are things people use from nature. We need some natural resources to survive.

➡ We need water to drink.

➡ We need air, water, soil, and sunlight to grow the food we eat.

➡ Trees and other plants also make the **oxygen** (air) we need to breathe.

Some natural resources do not keep us alive, but they are very useful. People make useful products with metals, such as cans from aluminum. People use oil, coal, and gas resources as **fuel**. These fuels help us to cook food, keep homes warm or cool, and make machines work.

5

We need to drink extra water when we exercise.

Water is one of the most important natural resources. We need to drink six to eight glasses of water a day to keep healthy. We use water for cooking, washing, and cleaning. Farmers use water to grow food, and we also use water in swimming pools.

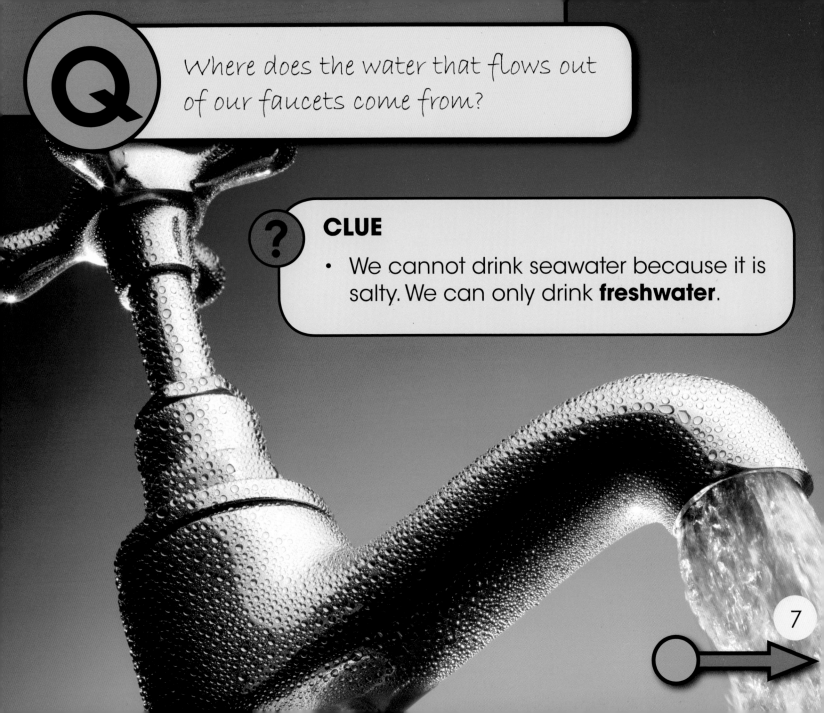

Q Where does the water that flows out of our faucets come from?

CLUE

- We cannot drink seawater because it is salty. We can only drink **freshwater**.

7

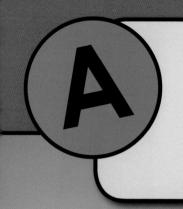**A** The water we drink comes from lakes, rivers, and **reservoirs**. These are all sources of **freshwater**. We also get freshwater from **aquifers**. These are layers of rock underground that hold water.

People dig reservoirs like this to store rain and water from rivers.

Most of the water from our faucets comes from reservoirs. Pipes carry the water from the reservoir to water treatment plants. The water is cleaned there. Then the water travels through long underground pipes to buildings, factories, and farms.

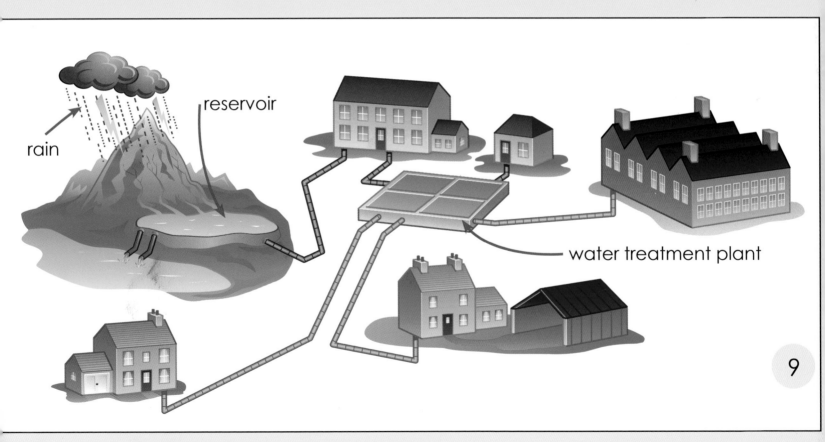

rain

reservoir

water treatment plant

Food Resources

Farmers use natural resources to grow food. We need to eat food to stay alive. We need to eat many different foods to get the **energy** and **nutrients** our bodies need to grow and stay healthy.

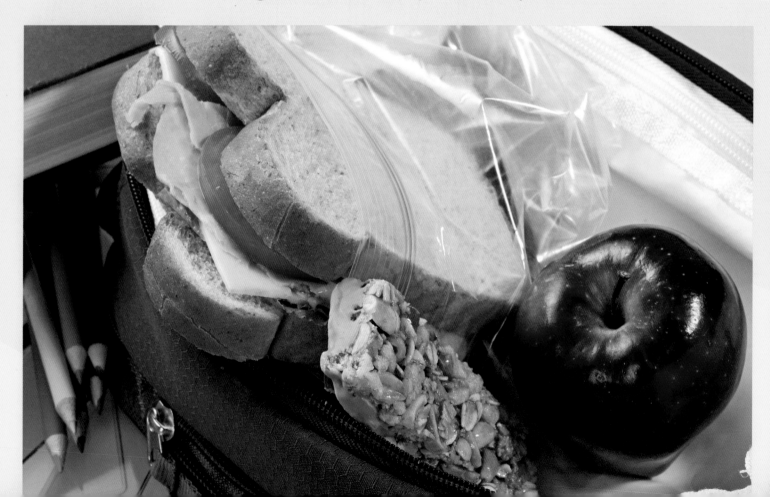

How does sunlight help to give us different foods?

CLUE

- What do plants need to grow?

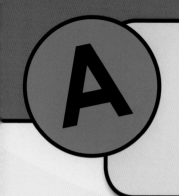

A Sunlight gives plants the **energy** they need to grow. Plants also need water to grow. We eat the plants that grow as food, or we get our food from other animals that eat plants.

1

⬆ The Sun is the source of all energy on Earth.

⬇ Plants trap the energy of the Sun. They use it to turn air and water into food.

2

Animals, including humans, eat plants to get energy.

3

4

People also eat foods that come from plant-eating animals.

13

The different parts of a plant have different jobs to do.

Stems hold up the leaves and flowers.

Leaves catch sunlight and make food for the plant.

Flowers make seeds that can grow into new plants.

Roots (underground) take in water from the soil.

For many plants, their fruits protect the seeds while they grow.

Q What plant parts can we eat?

? CLUE
- What parts of these plants can we eat?

We can eat all of the parts of plants. We eat different parts from different plants.

This chart shows some plant parts that we eat.

Plant part	Food name
Root	Carrot Parsnip Turnip
Leaves	Cabbage Lettuce Spinach
Stem	Rhubarb Celery Asparagus
Flower	Cauliflower Broccoli
Fruit	Apples Strawberries Plums
Seeds	Peas Fava beans Sunflower seeds

We eat some plant foods as they are. We can just wash an apple before eating it. Other foods are **processed**. For example, wheat **grains** (seeds) are crushed into flour. People use flour to make bread, pasta, and breakfast cereals.

Animal Foods

Farm animals need land to live on, air to breathe, and food to eat so they can grow and stay healthy. Farmers give animals water to drink and use water to grow food for the animals to eat. Most farm animals mainly eat plants, including grass, hay, corn, and other **grains**.

Hens produce eggs that we eat. We can eat chicken meat, too.

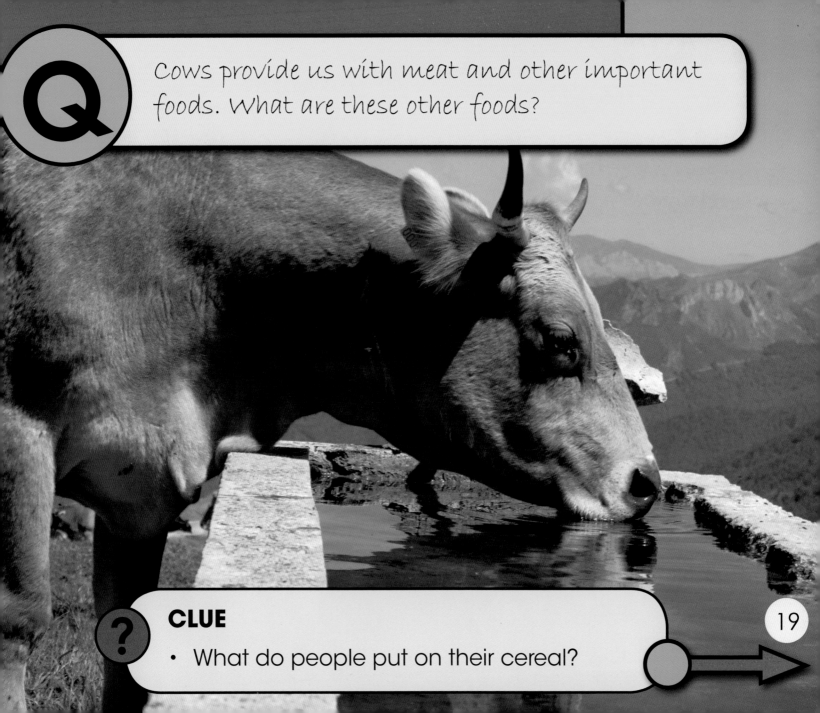

Q Cows provide us with meat and other important foods. What are these other foods?

CLUE

- What do people put on their cereal?

19

A

Cows produce milk that we can drink. People also use milk to make butter, cheese, and yogurt.

⬇ Foods made from milk are called dairy products.

Most milk is **pasteurized** before we drink it. This means it is heated to kill off bacteria and make it safe. Milk is **processed** in different ways to make dairy products like cheese and yogurt.

This man is separating milk into curds and whey in order to make cheese.

Where Food Grows

Different kinds of food plants grow best in different parts of the world because of **climate**. Wheat grows best in cooler, drier climates. Tropical fruits like bananas and mangoes grow in warmer, wetter climates.

↑ These bananas are growing in Uganda, in Africa.

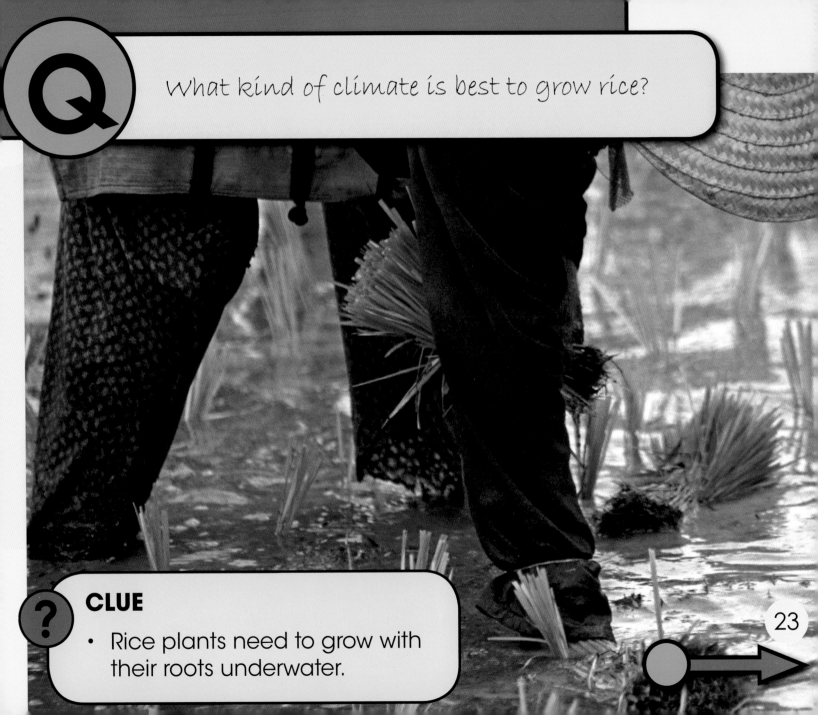

Q What kind of climate is best to grow rice?

CLUE
- Rice plants need to grow with their roots underwater.

23

A Rice grows in parts of the world that get a lot of rain in the rice-growing season. Asian countries like India have a wet and a dry season. During the wet **monsoon** season, rain fills the rice fields with water.

In some parts of the world, it is very sunny and hot and there is little rain all year round. Sometimes there is a **drought**. This is when there is so little rainfall for so long that the soil dries out and food plants die. This leaves people thirsty and hungry.

Earth's Fuels

People take coal, oil, and gas **fuels** from beneath Earth's surface. They dig coal from mines and drill deep underground for oil and gas. People mainly use coal and gas to make electricity in power stations.

This huge machine called a power shovel has been digging up coal from the ground.

Oil can be used to make many different things, including:

➧ gasoline to power cars and other vehicles

➧ plastic for thousands of different products, such as pens and toothbrushes

➧ **fertilizers** for farms.

Saving Natural Resources

People rely on different natural resources in many ways. We need to use natural resources carefully so there are enough for the future. Oil resources are running out. It takes a lot of oil to transport food across the world in trucks, ships, trains, and planes.

When people buy food that grows locally, less **fuel** is used to transport food from farm to store.

Some places have more natural resources than others. Sometimes this causes problems between countries—for example, if they have to share water. People need to find a way to use important resources fairly, so that everyone has a share of the resources they need.

⬆ Some places on Earth are short of water, so farmers try to plant **crops** that need very little water to grow well.

Checklist

Natural resources come from nature.

We need these natural resources to live:

⇒ air

⇒ soil

⇒ sunlight

⇒ water.

We use natural resources in different ways:

water to drink

water, air, sunlight, and soil to grow food

oil, coal, and gas to make electricity and power machines.

Glossary

aquifer underground layer of rock and sand that holds water

climate general conditions of weather in an area

crop plants that farmers grow and harvest to eat or to sell

drought long period of time with little or no rainfall

energy ability to do work, move, or change. There are different kinds of energy. People use energy from food to live and grow.

fertilizer powder, spray, or liquid that farmers put on soil to help plants grow

freshwater water that people can drink and use to wash and grow plants

fuel substance that people can burn to make heat or light or to power machines

grain seed

monsoon period of time when it rains very heavily. Monsoons happen during the summer over south and southeast Asia.

nutrient substance that is important for a living thing's health

oxygen gas in the air that people and other animals need to breathe

pasteurize heat milk in order to kill off harmful things like bacteria and mold that could make people sick

process change a material into something else in a series of stages. For example, oil is processed into different products before it can be used.

reservoir artificial (human-made) lake that holds water and stores it for future use

Index